New boots

Story by Annette Smith
Illustrations by Betty Greenhatch

Jack and Billy
went into the shop
with Mom.

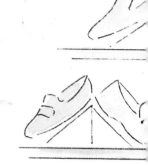

"Come and look at the boots,"
said Mom.
"I will get you some boots."

3

"I like the blue boots,"
said Jack.

"I like the red boots,"
said Billy.

5

Mom and Jack and Billy
went home with the boots.

"Dad! Dad!" shouted Jack.
"Mom got us some boots.
Look'"

Jack and Billy ran inside.

"I like your boots,"
said Dad.

9

"Your boots go in here,"
said Mom.
"They are for rainy days."

Billy looked at Mom.
"I like my red boots,"
he said.

"Jack! Billy!" said Dad.

"Are you hungry?

Come and eat."

13

"Here you are, Jack,"
 said Dad.
"Where is Billy?"

"Billy is on his bed," said Jack.
"He is asleep."

Jack said,

"Billy likes his red boots."